PRE-SCHOOL UPPERCASE ALPHABET

Fun-filled Activities

An imprint of Om Books International

The Letter A

Read aloud the name of each picture. Write A for the pictures names of which begin with the letter A.

Trace and write A.

A A A

The Letter B

Read aloud the name of each picture. Circle (O) all the pictures names of which begin with the **letter B**.

Trace and write B.

B B B

The Letter C

Read aloud the name of each picture. Tick (✓) all the pictures names of which begin with the **letter C**.

Trace and write C.

C C C

The Letter D

Read aloud the name of each picture. Write D for the pictures names of which begin with the letter D.

Trace and write D.

The Letter E

Read aloud the name of each picture. Circle (O) all the pictures names of which begin with the **letter E**.

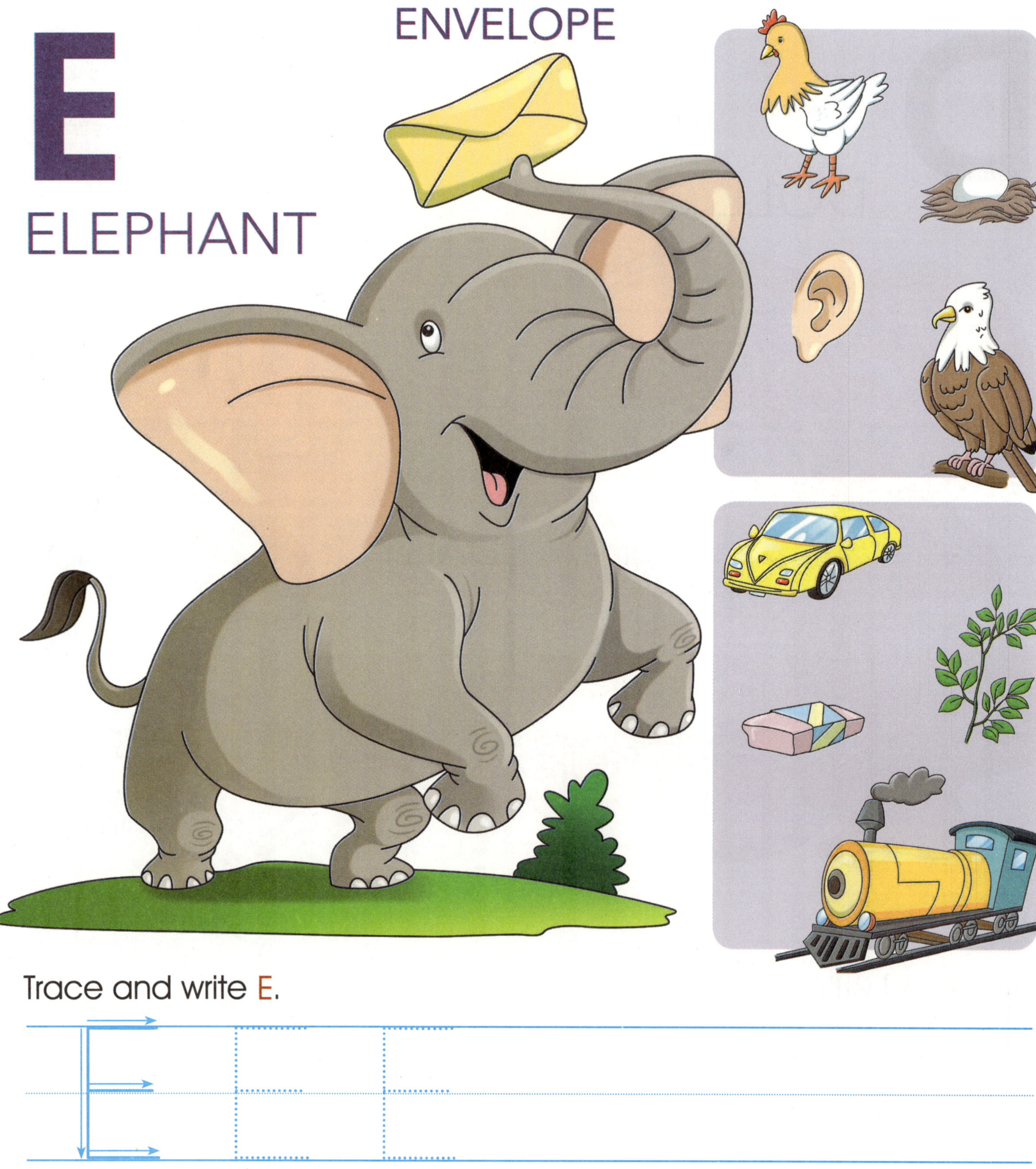

Trace and write E.

The Letter F

Read aloud the name of each picture. Tick (✓) all the pictures the names of which begin with the letter F.

Trace and write F.

The Letter G

Read aloud the name of each picture. Write G for the pictures names of which begin with the letter G.

G

GIRAFFE

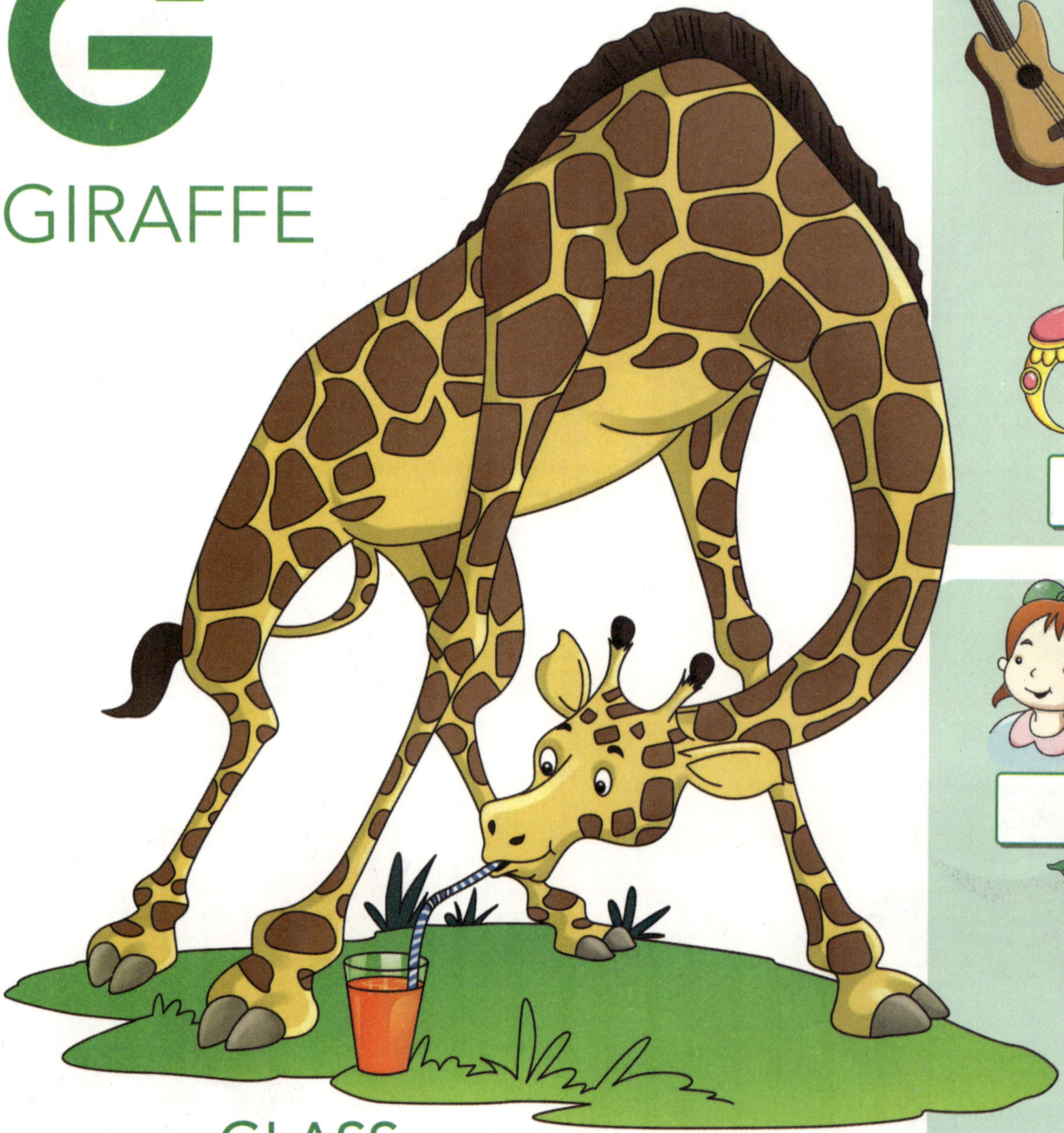

GLASS

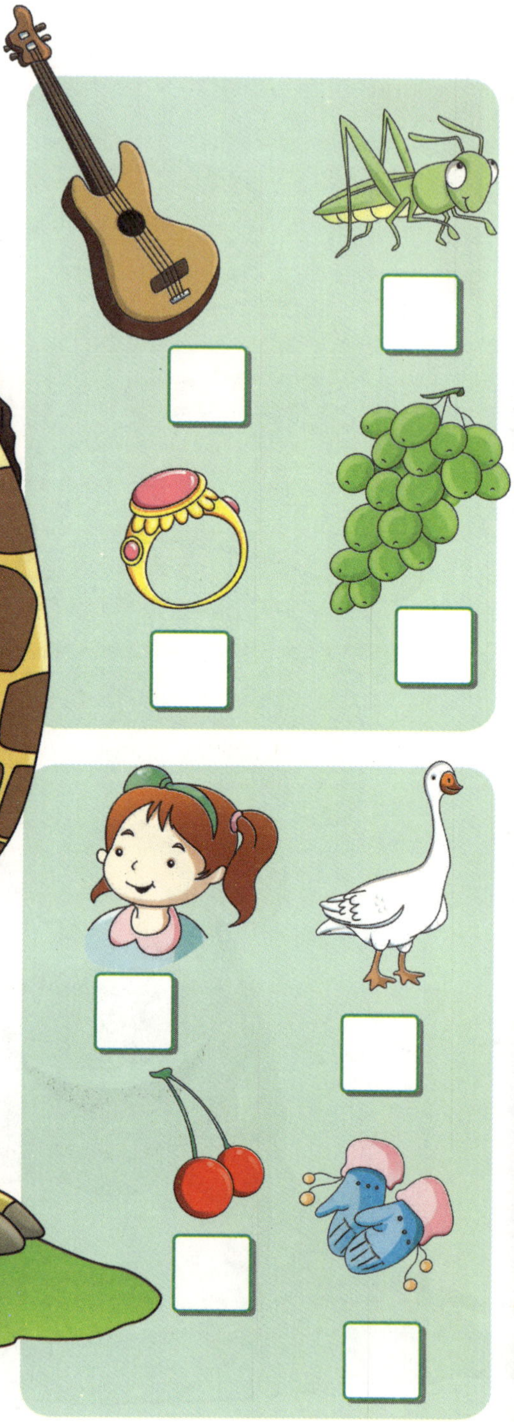

Trace and write G.

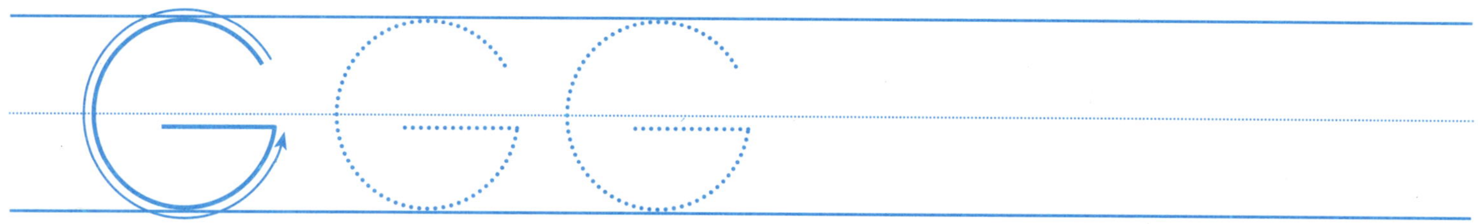

The Letter H

Read aloud the name of each picture. Circle (O) all the pictures names of which begin with the letter H.

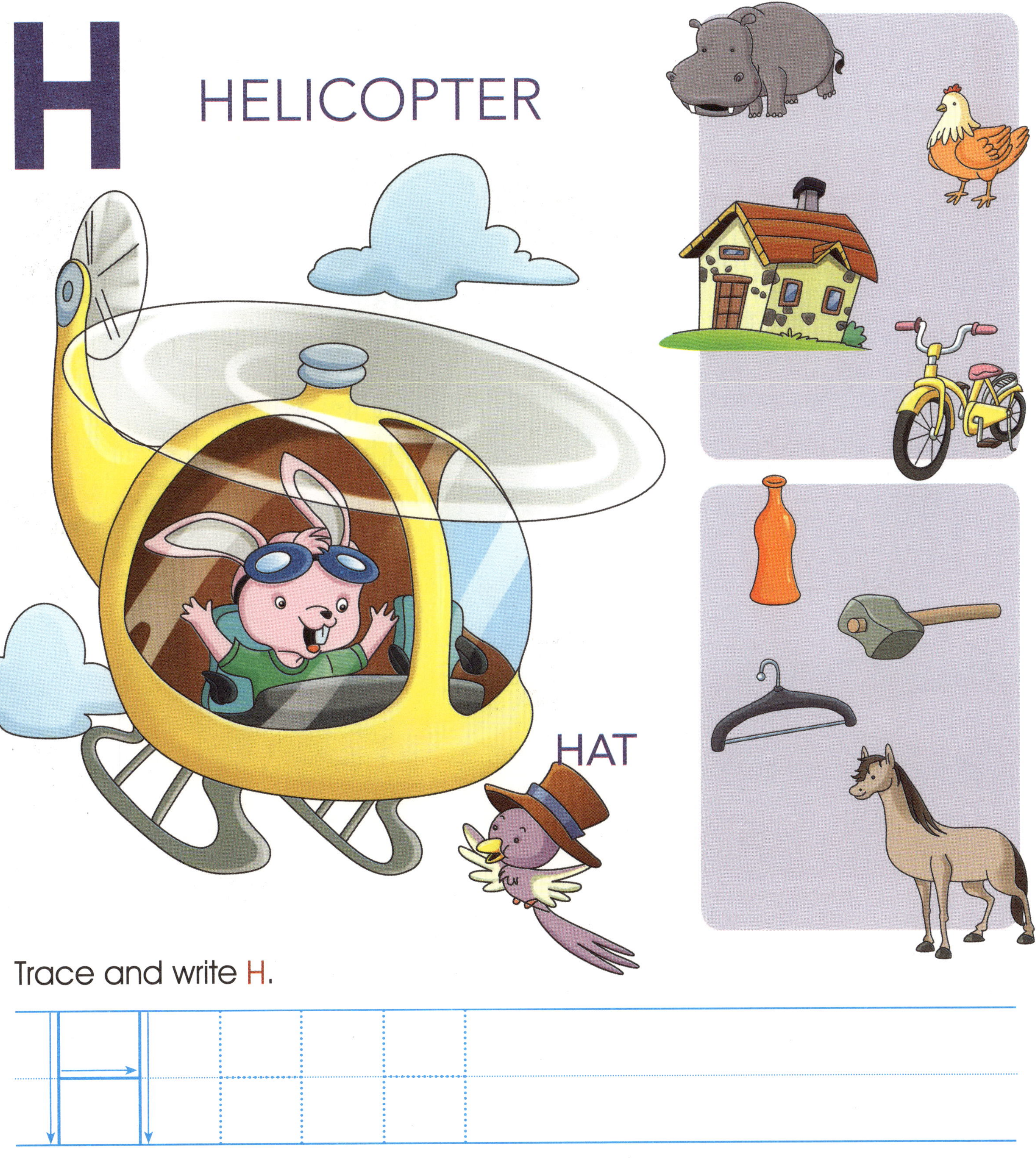

Trace and write H.

The Letter I

Read aloud the name of each picture. Tick (✓) all the pictures the names of which begin with the letter I.

Trace and write I.

Fun With Letters

Find and circle (O) the pictures names of which begin with the letters given below. Colour the scene.

How many did you find?

A ◯ B ◯ C ◯ D ◯ E ◯ F ◯ G ◯ H ◯ I ◯

The Letter J

Read aloud the name of each picture. Write J for the pictures names of which begin with the letter J.

Trace and write J.

J J J

The Letter K

Read aloud the name of each picture. Circle (O) all the pictures names of which begin with the letter K.

Trace and write K.

K K K

The Letter L

Read aloud the name of each picture. Tick (✓) all the pictures names of which begin with the letter L.

Trace and write L.

L

The Letter M

Read aloud the name of each picture. Write M for the pictures names of which begin with the letter M.

Trace and write M.

M M M

The Letter N

Read aloud the name of each picture. Circle (O) all the pictures names of which begin with the letter N.

Trace and write N.

The Letter O

Read aloud the name of each picture. Tick (✓) all the pictures names of which begin with the letter O.

O OCTOPUS

OAR

Trace and write O.

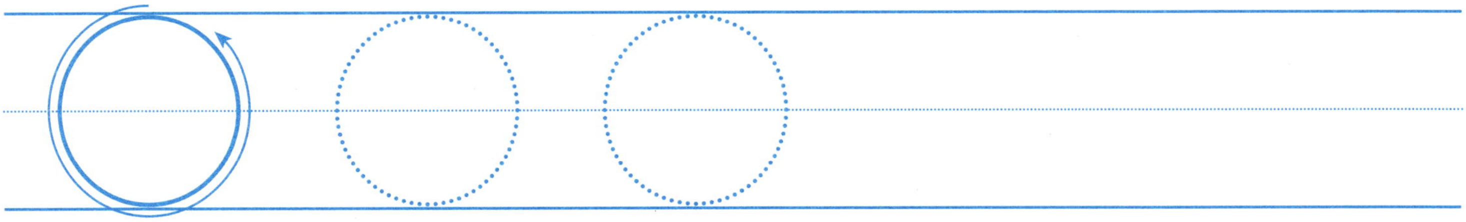

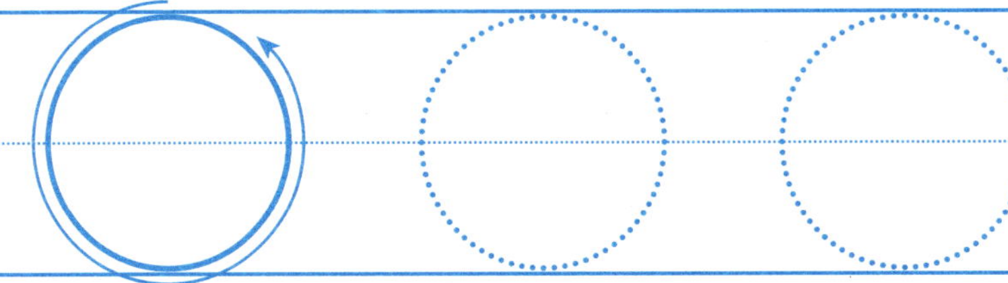

The Letter P

Read aloud the name of each picture. Write P for the pictures names of which begin with the letter P.

Trace and write P.

The Letter Q

Read aloud the name of each picture. Circle (O) all the pictures names of which begin with the letter Q.

Trace and write Q.

The Letter R

Read aloud the name of each picture. Tick (✓) all the pictures names of which begin with the letter R.

Trace and write R.

R R R

Fun With Letters

Write the first letter of the name of the first picture. Then circle (O) the picture with same beginning letter

The Letter S

Read aloud the name of each picture. Write S for the pictures names of which begin with the letter S.

S

SHEEP

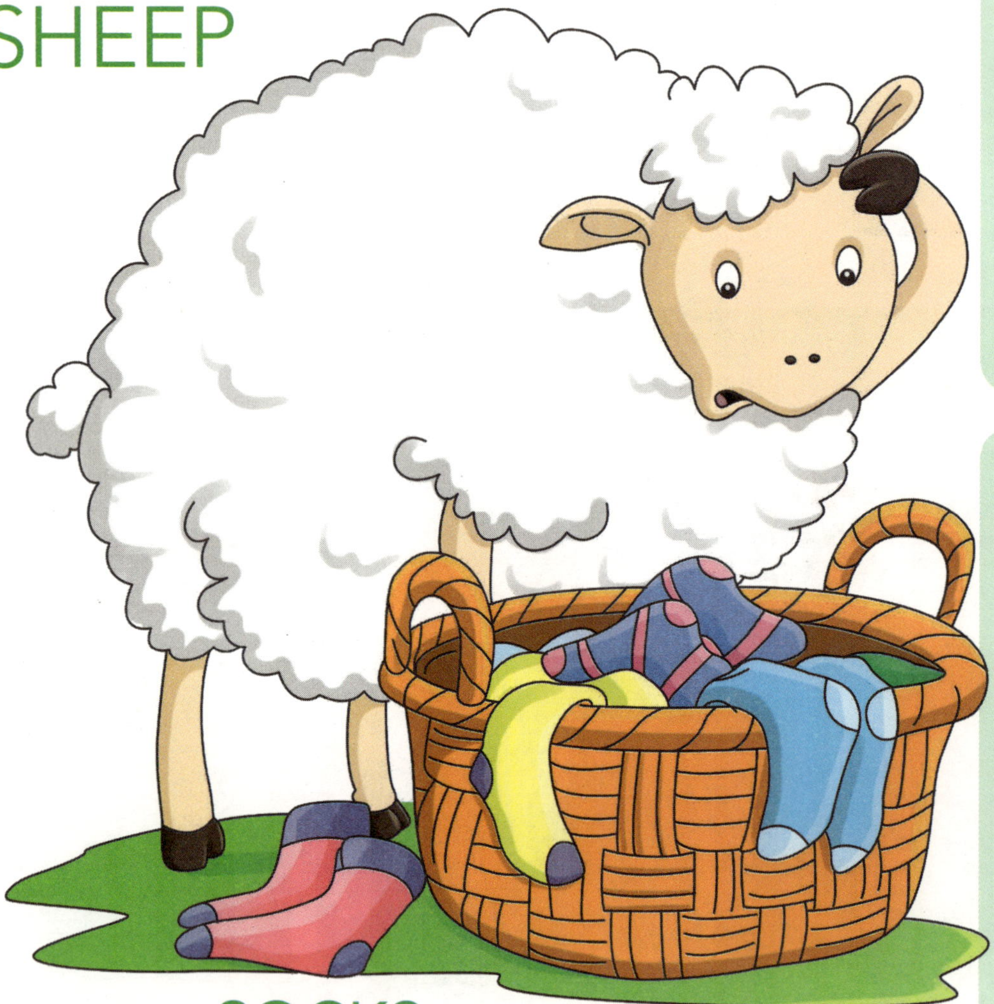

SOCKS

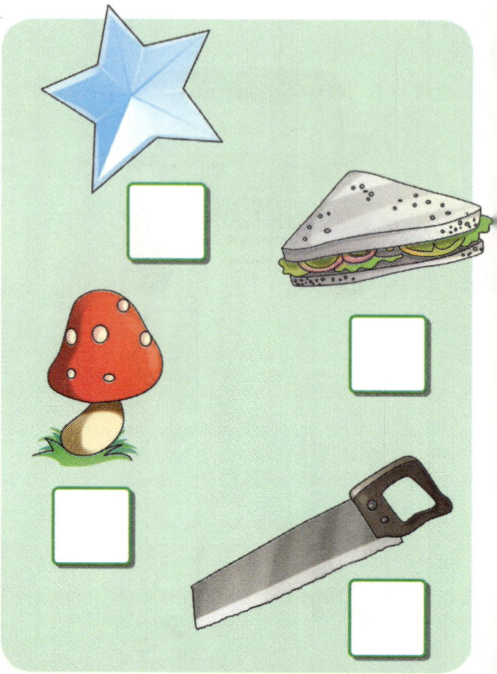

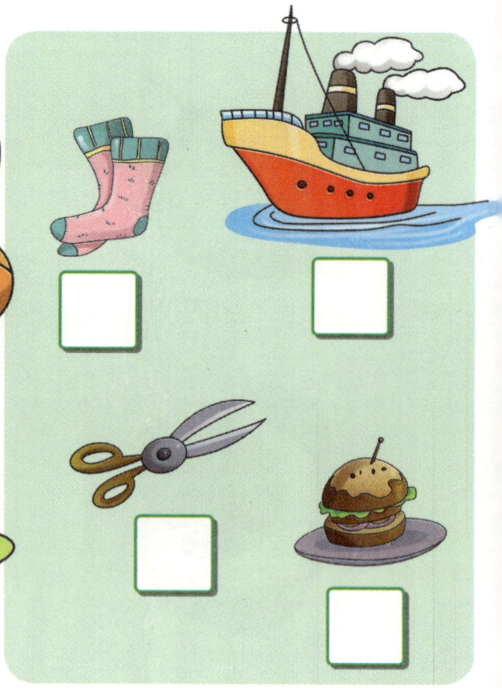

Trace and write S.

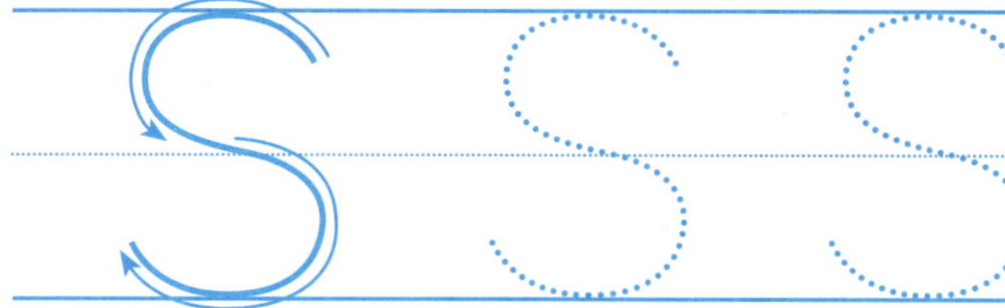

The Letter T

Read aloud the name of each picture. Circle (O) all the pictures names of which begin with the letter T.

Trace and write T.

The Letter U

Read aloud the name of each picture. Tick (✓) all the pictures names of which begin with the letter U.

Trace and write U.

The Letter V

Read aloud the name of each picture. Write V for the pictures names of which begin with the letter V.

Trace and write V.

V V V

The Letter W

Read aloud the name of each picture. Circle (O) all the pictures names of which begin with the letter W.

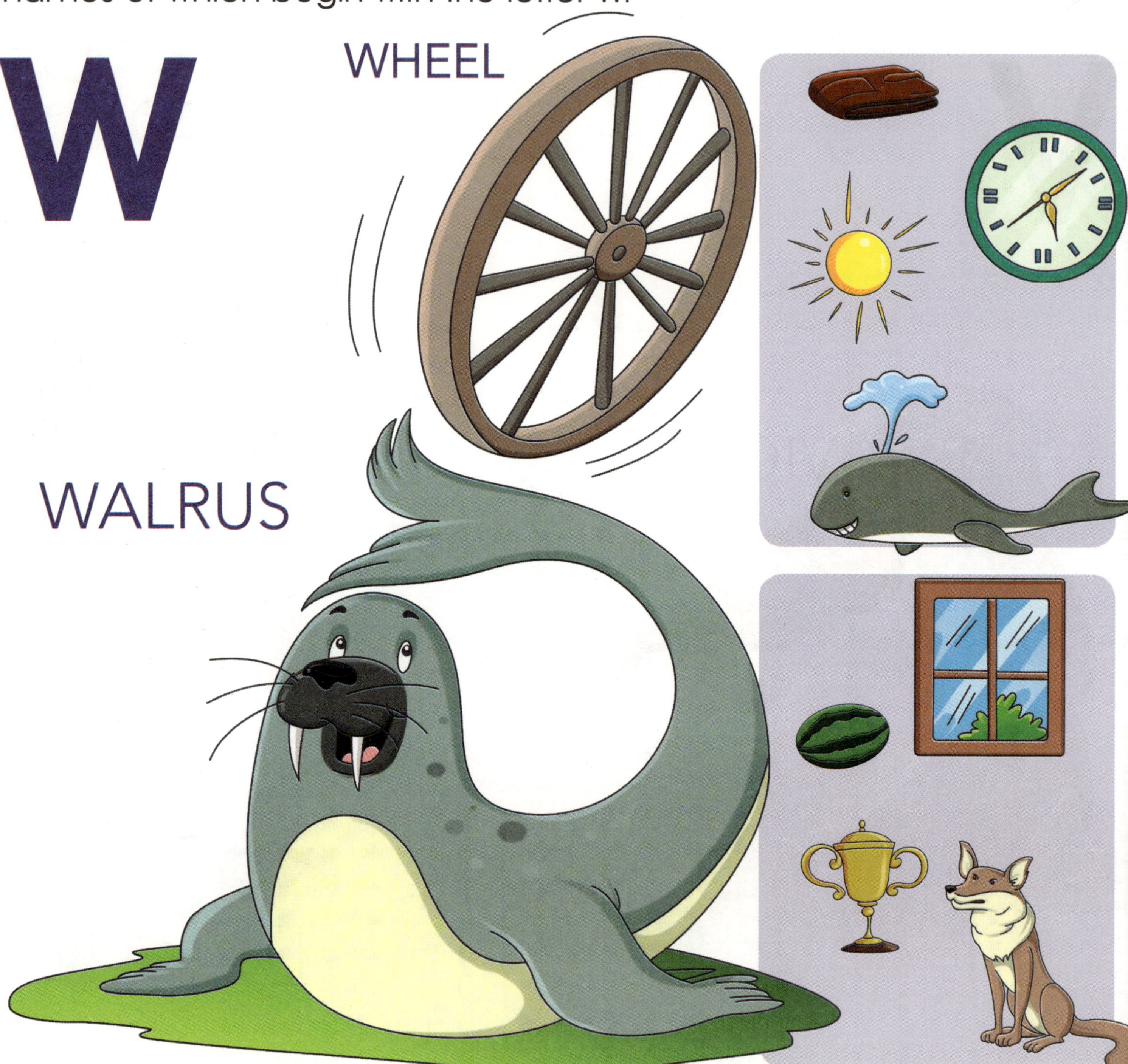

Trace and write W.

The letter X

Read aloud the name of each picture. Tick (✓) all the pictures names of which begin with the letter X.

Trace and write X.

X X X

The Letter Y

Read aloud the name of each picture. Write Y for the pictures names of which begin with the letter Y.

Trace and write Y.

Y Y Y

The Letter Z

Read aloud the name of each picture. Circle (O) all the pictures names of which begin with the letter Z.

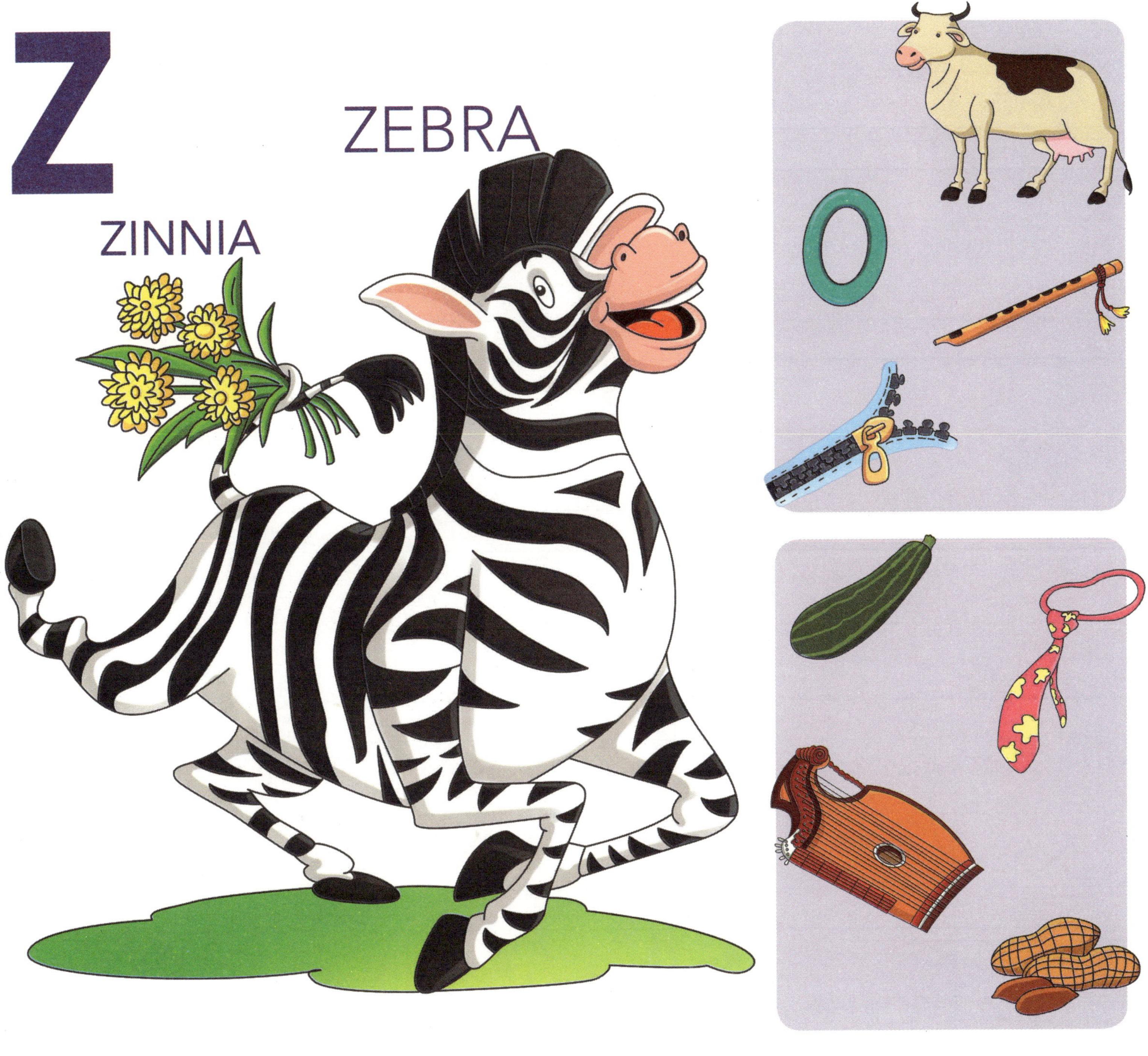

Trace and write Z.

Fun With Letters

Get, set, go and trace these letters. Say each letter as you move.

A B C D

E F G H

I J K L

M N O P

Q R S T

U V W X

Y Z

Answer Key

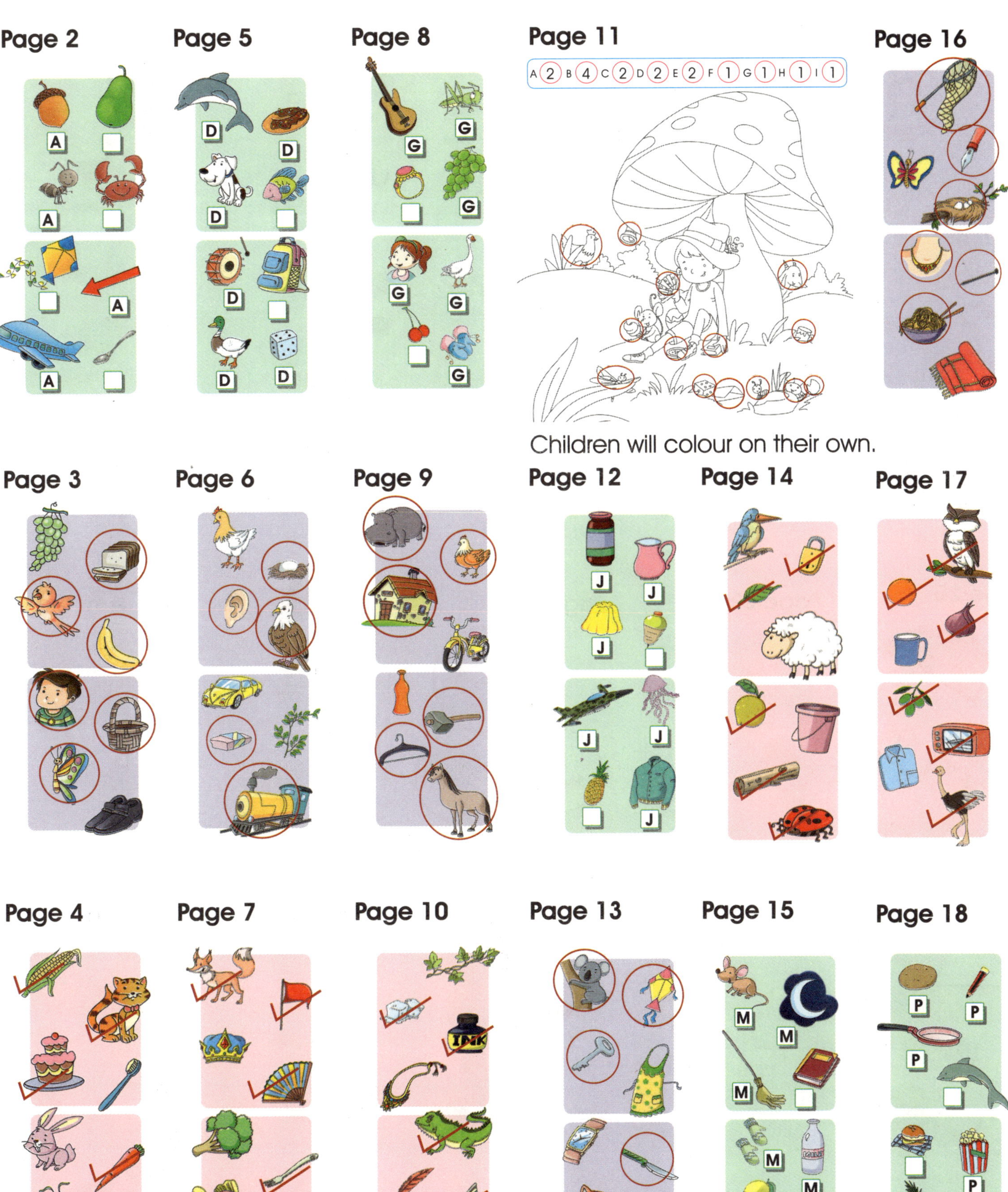

Children will colour on their own.

Answer Key

Page 19

Page 21

Page 24

Page 27

Page 25

Page 28

Page 20

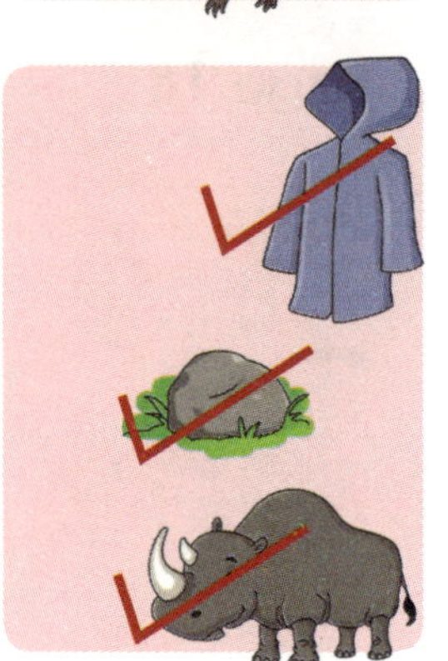

Page 22

Page 23

Page 26

Page 29

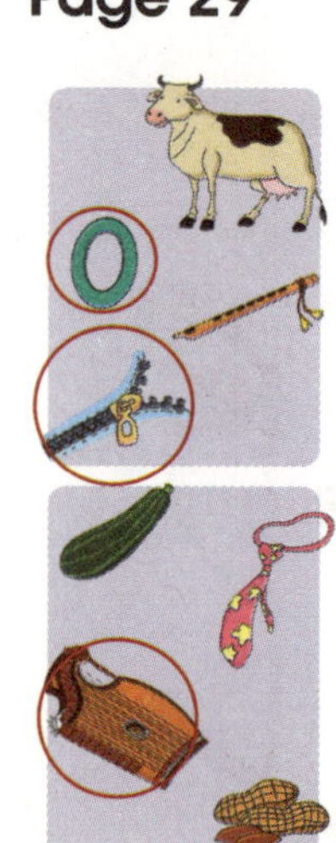